Methodism and Bible

Holiness

by

Ebenezer Myers

First Fruits Press
Wilmore, Kentucky
c2015

Methodism and Bible Holiness by Ebenezer Myers.

First Fruits Press, ©2015
Previously published: Lenoir, N.C. : Ebenezer Myers, 1958.

ISBN: 9781621712657 (print), 9781621712664 (digital), 9781621712671 (kindle)

Digital version at
http://place.asburyseminary.edu/firstfruitsheritagematerial/110/

Myers, Ebenezer.
    Methodism and Bible holiness / Ebenezer Myers.
    Fourth edition.
    56 pages : portrait ; 21 cm.
    Wilmore, Ky. : First Fruits Press, ©2015.
    Reprint. Previously published: Lenoir, N.C. : Ebenezer Myers, [1958].
    ISBN: 9781621712657 (pbk.)
    1. Holiness 2. Perfection. 3. Methodist Church – Doctrines. I. Title.
BT766 .M94 2015   234.8

Cover design by Wesley Wilcox

asburyseminary.edu
800.2ASBURY
204 North Lexington Avenue
Wilmore, Kentucky 40390

First Fruits
THE ACADEMIC OPEN PRESS OF ASBURY SEMINARY

First Fruits Press
The Academic Open Press of Asbury Theological Seminary
204 N. Lexington Ave., Wilmore, KY 40390
859-858-2236
first.fruits@asburyseminary.edu
asbury.to/firstfruits

METHODISM
and
BIBLE HOLINESS

✝

EBENEZER MYERS

Methodism and Bible Holiness

By Ebenezer Myers
210 Vance St.
Lenoir, N. C.

FOURTH EDITION—DECEMBER 1958

PREFACE

This little book is written and sent forth in love for all my brethren; and in the interest of the cause of righteousness in general; and especially in defense of the doctrine and experience of holiness; and for the protection and defense of the holiness preachers, and more especially the young men who are coming into our Conferences who believe in holiness and who are put to severe tests by antiholiness preachers and bishops.

It is written in the same honest, sincere way that I have preached the gospel for seventy-one years. Some of it is sharp but things must be sharp to stick and with barbs enough to hold them fast.

EBENEZER MYERS

Lenoir, N. C., 1958

CONTENTS

4

CHAPTER I

A BRIEF HISTORY OF THE DOCTRINE OF HOLINESS IN THE WORLD

THE DOCTRINE IN THE OLD TESTAMENT

God created man pure and holy, very good; no flaws or imperfections; but man did not keep his first estate of holiness, but sinned and became unholy and sinful, but God's plan for man was holiness of heart and life and he went about carrying out his plans and purposes for a holy people. In Ex. 19:6 God calls his people "A kingdom of priests, and a holy nation" and quoted by Peter in I Peter 2:9, shows that it was God's purpose to raise up and use a holy people; we can see how Israel failed him, but that did not alter God's purpose.

God did succeed with a few of them in making them holy; for all we know, Abel, the first martyr, was one of them; we know that Enoch was one of the holy men, for the record says that he walked with God for three hundred years.

A number of men and women down through Old Testament times appear to have the experience but there are a few that we can see where they received the experience. Abraham at the time of the divided offering and the change of his name proves it. Isaac seems to have some of the marks of a holy man. Jacob's case very clear: was converted at Bethel and sanctified at Peniel, with the all night wrestle with the man, or angel, of the Covenant, and it was the angel that wrestled with him and prevailed only when he

5

had put his hip out of place, and in Gen. 48:3 and 16 he tells of the two experiences bearing testimony in the 16th verse to holiness in these words: "The Angel that delivered me *from all evil.*"

David in Psa. 51 prays for sanctification, confessing his need of it, and seems to have obtained it, for his after life bears it out. Isaiah in Chapter 6 is a clear case of obtaining holiness and the wonderful life of Service and the clear vision of prophecy shows it to have been real: Jeremiah, Ezekiel and Daniel all seem to be of the same type; with some of the minor prophets and other Old Testament saints showing the same kind of life. Elijah seemed to be full of the fire of God, and Elisha asked for and obtained the double portion of the same spirit and his after life showed that he obtained it and how it sustained him amid the trials that he met and the works that he did. John the Baptist had the experience which so wonderfully prepared him for his work, enabling him to recognize the Messiah whom he had come to introduce to the world. Old Simeon and Anna in the temple had the experience enabling them to recognize the Messiah as he came to the temple for his first worship, and behold these saints meet and worship Him although He is but a babe. Mary the mother of Jesus no doubt had the experience and was permitted to worship her own baby, the only mother in the world who was justifiable in worshipping her own babe, although no doubt many have done so.

Moses, the man with whom God could talk face to face, and whom God honored to give his people and the world the law, had the gracious experience in rich abundance. Was it at the burning bush he got the experience?

CHAPTER II

The Doctrine of Holiness in the New Testament

Like the waters of Ezekiel's vision, this doctrine and experience beginning in a small way back there with the beginning of the race, enlarging as it flowed till the new dispensation, when the doctrine and experience of holiness burst forth in its fullness at Pentecost, the stage of Ezekiel's vision, "Waters to swim in which could not be waded," had arrived, the noonday of gospel grace. It was called by John the Baptist in Matt. 3:11, 12 the baptism of the Holy Ghost, saying "He shall baptize you with the Holy Ghost and with fire; whose fan is in his hand and he will thoroughly purge his floor and gather his wheat into his garner; but he will burn up the chaff with unquenchable fire." John is speaking prophetically and describes the work of the Holy Spirit in his sanctifying power.

Jesus takes up the same message in Acts 1:4, 5 "For John truly baptized with water; but ye shall be baptized with the Holy Ghost not many days hence." And in verse 8, same chapter, "But ye shall receive power after the Holy Ghost is come upon you; and ye shall be witnesses unto me both in Jerusalem and in all Judea and in Samaria and unto the uttermost parts of the earth." This of course was to be only 10 days off at Pentecost.

Jesus had promised in John 4th and 16th chapters the coming of the Holy Ghost who would do the baptizing and in the 17th chapter of John he prayed for this baptism to come upon them, but called it sanctification, verse 17. "Sanctify them through thy truth; thy word is truth." Verse

19, "And for their sakes I sanctify that they also may be sanctified through the truth." And in verse 29, "Neither pray I for these alone, but for them also which shall believe on me through their word." The prayer includes every believer down to the end of the age, not just a general prayer, but a special prayer that every one should be sanctified, and whoever pulls back and does not co-operate with him and let this prayer be answered in his own sanctification misses the glory of it.

So Pentecost was the fulfillment of the prophecy and the answer to Jesus' prayer for the Apostles and early disciples, and all believers should let the prayer be answered in their behalf by seeking sanctification.

This Pentecostal experience of the baptism of the Holy Spirit as the stream of full salvation continued to flow on through the Apostolic age and for many years afterward, until the momentum slowed down and was almost lost in the desert sands of a backslidden church as it went into the dark ages; but we see occasional signs of it when saints like Madam Guyon, Archbishop Fenelon and St. Francis of Assisi and others shone out in the darkness.

Martin Luther resurrected or rediscovered the doctrine of justification by faith, but it remained for John and Charles Wesley to rediscover and establish the doctrine and experience of sanctification or Christian perfection, or holiness, for they used all three terms synonymously.

Wesley had the doctrine of Christian perfection settled in his mind long before he was converted at Aldersgate, and when he discovered in his conversion that salvation was by faith and not by the works of the law, he began seeking sanctification by faith and the twenty-third day after his conversion he was sanctified. He tells his experience as follows: "I mourned day and night in agony to be thoroughly sanctified. On the twenty-third day after my justification I found a total change, together with a clear witness that the blood of Jesus cleanses from all unrighteousness." Again he says: "A pleasing thought passed through my mind that I was saved from the remains of all sin. As yet I have felt no return thereof." Again he says: "For months I have felt as if in the possession of perfect love, not a moment's desire for anything but God."

Then on January 1, following this experience, he with Charles, Whitfied, and four others of the preachers and sixty of the brethren at a love feast and all night prayer meeting at Fetter Lane, the Holy Spirit came upon them at three o'clock in the morning with Pentecostal power. And then followed field preaching and the greatest revival since Pentecost. (See McTyeire's History of Methodism, page 147.)

So the doctrine being thus repossessed was so strongly and intelligently preached, and incorporated into the organization and doctrine of the church that it has never been eradicated, and for more than a hundred years all the bishops and perhaps all the preachers preached it, and pressed it on the people and a large per cent of the people obtained and lived the experience; but about the end of the first hundred years the church began to turn away from it, as the preachers coming out of the colleges and schools of religion ceased to get the experience and preach the doctrine. The schools did it.

The source of this decline was not the common people or the preachers themselves but the schools, as they began to feel that education was the most important thing; and then this spirit has grown in the church till today the major emphasis is on education; the thing has happened according to Jude 19: "These be they who separate themselves, sensual, having not the spirit."

The word translated sensual there means intellectual, but which ends up in sensuality, as the balance of the verse says, "having not the spirit," as the Holy Spirit is the only power that can save us from sensuality.

Men with the greatest and best trained intellects may be devils, as we see many in the world today.

So the modernistic church of today with its great pretentions to intellectuality is failing to produce a spiritual membership; and sensuality seems to be possessing the membership; liquor drinking, card playing, dancing, selling beer, wine and liquor, Sunday golfing, Sunday joy riding, parks and swimming pools well attended by church members on Sunday, besides the lower forms of evil, adultery and uncleanness. In fact there seems to be little difference between church members and the world of those who are not members.

Thus we can see the fruits of the rejection of holiness with its high standards, and experience of power to overcome these evils.

The Holiness people, although most of them from the lower walks of life, have a much higher standard than do the wealthy, cultured members of our first churches; the fact is that the rejection of holiness has led to the awful state of the church today and largely responsible for world conditions.

CHAPTER III

GOD'S TWO GREAT DRAMAS

This doctrine of holiness is seen in two of God's holy dramas; the deliverance of the children of Israel from Egypt into the promised land; Egypt, bondage to sin; Pharoah, the devil; the crossing the Red Sea, conversion; the travels in the wilderness, Christian life before sanctification; the crossing of the Jordan, sanctification; and the Canaan life, the state of holiness, with victory over all enemies, and they had that victory as long as they obeyed the Lord.

Another drama is the life and experience of Job. The whole book of Job is an account of this drama; it makes no difference who wrote it nor when it was written; I have read much of what critics have said about this book and its author, but after all I believe that Job wrote it himself; eminently fitted as the instrument of God for writing it, knew all the facts and lived after this to see his descendants to the fourth generation. There is nothing that I can see that is inconsistent with his writing it; and while it is written as a drama, all the characters' names are given and some of them are verified by history, which cannot be said of fiction, so it is drama. God's holy drama enacted and written to prove and make very plain one of the greatest doctrines of the Bible.

But what is it? It is the doctrine and experience of Christian perfection. God starts out with his perfect man, that is, perfect in the Christian graces, not perfect physically or intellectually, but in God's grace. God said three times that he was perfect, Job 1:1, 8 and 2:3. He points out to the devil this perfect man, then the devil began to do his worst, as

God gave him permission; first, his wealth and his children went in a day; second, health went and instead great bodily afflictions; then friends forsook him; then his wife turned against him, turned traitor to God as well as to her husband; then his three friends came to comfort him, sat for some time studying his case and coming to the conclusion that he was suffering for some great sin, they commenced to accuse him and kept it up, taking all the arguments they could muster to prove to him that he was a sinner; but Job had the experience and the inner witness to it, and nothing could move him from it. So he constantly maintained his integrity and innocence of the charges they brought against him. The record says "in all this Job sinned not nor charged God foolishly." God wonderfully vindicated Job in his course and brought all those who failed to stand by him under conviction, made Eliphaz, Zophar and Bildad make an offering, and he had Job pray for them. Then God brought Job out of the dark tunnel through which he had gone, giving him great victory over it all; gave him twice as much property as he had at the beginning, as many children as he had before, and allowed him to see the fourth generation of his descendants. Now see his persecutors; holiness has always had its persecutors, and these are not the world but professors of religion; his wife, neighbors, friends in the neighborhood, and his three prominent friends who had come to comfort him. All these claimed to know God and to be his friends, but the "carnal mind is enmity against God" and as long as there is any of it, it will manifest itself; but God will give victory to his holy ones if they remain true; and Job's case proves that they can be true.

II Tim. 3:12. "Yea and all that will live godly in Christ Jesus shall suffer persecution." You can profess religion, join the church and go along in a smooth way without suffering persecution but when you undertake to go all the way with God in a life of holiness, "live holy," the devil will see that you get your share of persecution. Many preachers, and those who would like to be effective Christian workers, when faced with a whole consecration and what it implies, refuse to pay the price, and dry up and get nowhere; the self denial, and crucifixion of the old man is too much for them. When a preacher begins to realize that the holiness haters in the Conference will keep him out of the big appointments and that he will face this through his entire ministry, it is no small thing; but my brother it pays to go on with God. I have no regrets that I did it; and if I had it to do again I would do the same way, only I might go into the Nazarene Church where I would have more liberty, as many are doing.

CHAPTER IV

Entire Sanctification from the Standpoint of Methodism

I am writing three short papers on the doctrine of entire sanctification or holiness, one on the doctrine from the standpoint of Methodism, one from the standpoint of the Bible, and one from the standpoint of experience.

I was reared in the Presbyterian Church, was converted at eighteen years of age, in a Methodist revival, and after studying the doctrines of the different churches for about four months I found I was a Methodist, and went and joined the Methodist Church at Franklin, N. C., my home town. The first Methodist literature I read was the Methodist Armour and Wesley's Sermons, which were loaned me by the pastor of the Methodist Church and some good Methodist neighbors. When I joined conference I was given in my course of study, among others, the works of Wesley, Watson, Fletcher and Clarke. I saw in all these that the doctrine of entire sanctification was taught as a second work of grace instantaneously given and attainable by consecration and faith. But the preachers around me were opposing such a doctrine, and preaching the Zinzendorfian heresy that we are sanctified when we are justified, or growth theory, and young and untrained as I was, I thought they ought to know better than I. And so I drifted in after them till I had preached for five years, when one day the now sainted Dr. G. H. Detwiler in a very simple and quiet way led me into the truth that we are sanctified as well as justified by faith, "not by works lest any man should boast," and if by faith why not have it now? I began to read the Bible in the light of his explanation and saw clearly the doctrine in the Bible, and have never wavered a hair's breadth from the doctrine from that day till this, but grow stranger in it every day.

The question arises, what is the teaching of our church on this doctrine today? There is no question with any intellingent Methodist preacher or layman about what it was with Wesley, Fletcher, Watson, Clarke, Asbury and all the Methodist fathers; every intelligent young man among us knows that they taught that entire sanctification was a definite second work of grace. But some want to claim that Mr. Wesley gave up the doctrine before he died, but this is a great mistake. In his writings we find it within a few months of his death. I suppose as long as he wrote at all he wrote on his subject, for this was the hub of his teaching and his whole religious life. Two years before his death, 1790, (he died in 1792) he wrote, "This doctrine is the grand despositum which God has lodged with the people called Methodists; and he appears to have raised us up chiefly for the sake of propagating this." And it is a fact that all the others mentioned clung to the doctrine to the end of their lives.

But let us see what the doctrine of our church on this point is today, and we are not to rely on what is being preached and taught by church leaders, bishops, presiding elders, college presidents, or pastors on this subject; we ar not to go to these for the doctrine, although they may be right (for some are right and some are wrong), but to the standards of Methodism—"to the law and to the testimony."

It is in our discipline, it is in our hymnal, and it is in our course of study. If this was the teaching of the fathers, why is it not the teaching of the church at the present time? When was it abrogated or superseded by something else?

What General Conference, or by what authority was the change made? There has been no change in our doctrinal standards; in fact, they cannot be changed without seriously affecting the whole church, for this is the chief doctrinal cornerstone of the whole church. The only change that has been made is by the preachers and teachers themselves, as they have left or run over our doctrinal standards for their own notions, just as the higher critics are doing today— there is no change in our doctrine but a change in practice, and I propose to show how this change has come about. I want first to introduce Dr. Lovick Pierce, father of Bishop Pierce, who preached more than seventy-five years. I quote from his little book, "Entire Sanctification, How It Was Lost from the Church and How It Must Be Regained." On page 22 we have this statement: "Well now for comparative facts; I say in the first twenty years of my ministry ninety-five per cent of our people were all alive and awake to this full salvation idea, and pressing it, and often finding it as manifestly as they did conversion, but now in the seventy-fourth year of my ministry I think I am fearfully safe in saying seventy-five per cent of our members are living in antinomian indifference to entire sanctification, neither believing in it, praying for it, nor really desiring it, and yet our leading men are saying Methodism has never seen a day when it was in better condition. They will excuse me for dissenting. It is meet that I should say right here that if we would resume our original special vocation, the spreading of scriptural holiness over these lands by preaching it, living it, professing it and enforcing it in our discipline, we would see the glory of God as never before; but alas for us, we left God just when He was our co-worker in spreading scriptural holiness over these broad American lands."

Dr. Pierce shows clearly in this little book how so large

a per cent of the church has lost the doctrine and experience and how it may and must be regained, as is seen in this brief that I have quoted. Let the reader get the book from our publishing house and read it; the price is only 15 cents.

Next I introduce the bishops of the church in their address to the General Conference in 1824. They said: "If Methodists give us the doctrine of entire sanctification, or suffer it to become a dead letter, we are a fallen people. Holiness is the main cord that binds us together; relax this and you loosen the whole system. This will appear more evident if we recall to mind the original design of Methodism, it was to raise up and preserve a holy people. This was the principal object which Mr. Wesley had in view. To this end all the doctrines believed and preached by the Methodists tend."

Were they right? Is this a clear statement of an authoritative band of witnesses?

If these bishops should suddenly come back to earth and view the Methodist Church and especially should they see the churches with no prayer meetings and no Sunday night services, but instead card playing and dancing in the churches, they would no doubt say, "We are a fallen church."

But I want to introduce a great Methodist scholar, Dr. John McClintock of Drew Theological Seminary, who said in the closing words of his centenary sermon in 1866: "Knowing exactly what I say, and taking the full responsibility of it, I repeat, we are the only church in history from the apostles' times till now that has put forth the very elemental thought the great pervading idea of the whole book of God from the beginning to the end, the holiness of the human soul, heart and will. It may be called fanaticism, but dear friends, this is our mission. If we keep to that the triumphs of the next century will throw those of the past into the shade. There is our mission; there is our glory; there is our power; and there shall be the ground of our triumph! God keep us true." But have we been true? Only a few have. The great bulk of our preachers and people have forsaken it.

But I bring up other authoritative witnesses. The bishops of the M. E. Church, South, in their quadrennial address in 1874 said: "Extensive revivals of religion have crowned the labors of our preachers, and the life-giving energy of the gospel in the conversion of sinners and sanctification of believers has been seldom more apparent among us. The boon of Wesleyan Methodism as we received it from the fathers has not been forfeited in our hands." This was signed by Bishop Robert Paine, George F. Pierce, H. H. Kavanaugh, W. M. Wightman, E. M. Marvin, D. S. Doggett, H. N. McTyeire and J. C. Keener. Some statements in this are made by some of our holiness evangelists that some of the preachers of today like to ridicule—"Sinners converted and believers sanctified." They show shallowness of religion and smallness of intellect by such criticism, for it is the criticism not only of the brother who makes the report of his meeting, but of the whole church from the beginning.

Twenty years later in 1894, the bishops of the M. E. Church, South, said in their address to the General Conference: "The privilege of believers to attain unto a state of entire sanctification, or perfect love, and to abide therein is a well known teaching of Methodism. Witnesses to this experience have never been wanting in the church, though few in comparison with the whole membership. Among them have been men and women of beautiful consistency and seraphic ardor—jewels of the church. Let the doctrine still be preached and the experience still be testified." Is this good authority? Does this sound like it had been exchanged for Zinbendorfism or any other ism?

Once more, and more united authority, the Centennial Conference of American Methodism in Baltimore in 1884 said in reaffirming the faith of the whole church, in all its separate branches: "We remind you, brethren, that the mission of Methodism is to promote holiness. It is not a sentiment or any emotion, but a principle inwrought in the heart, the culmination of God's work in us, followed by a consecrated life. In all the borders of Methodism this doctrine is preached, and the experience of sanctification is urged. We beseech you, brethren, stand by your standards on this subject." You see that this conference of American Methodism recognized the standards of Methodism on this subject. Is this not sufficient to show that we have had these standards all these years and that those who teach anything else have simply left or run over the standards?

But I said it was in the discipline of our church. It is in the baptismal services where we pray for the sanctification of the candidate and where we pray that the old man may be so buried that the new man may be raised up in him. Our doctrine of holiness has its roots in our article of religion on original sin. "Original sin standeth not in the following of Adam as the Pelagians do vainly talk, but it is the corruption of the nature of *every man* that it is naturally engendered of the offspring of Adam whereby man is very far gone from original righteousness, and of his own nature inclined to evil and that continually." But I will not take space for the discussion of this, as that would be too long for a newspaper article.

But I notice only one more place in the discipline, and

that is the question involved in the first four questions that every Methodist must answer in the affirmative when he is received into the annual conference. These questions involve the doctrine of entire sanctification or perfect love as taught by our church from the beginning, and were put there to keep a preacher from the connection that would not get the experience and preach the doctrine. It is the guard at the conference door to protect the church from the impostor.

Here are the four questions:

1. Have you faith in Christ? Involving not only doctrine of faith but experimental faith. He has been a member and a preacher for a number of years and should have saving faith as well as sound doctrine.

Are you going on to perfection? We know that this means perfection in love only as any other perfection does not belong to man, but the experience of sanctification or perfect love is for man and we say we are going on to it, not merely toward it but actually to get the experience, and this is involved in the next two questions: "Do you expect to be made perfect in love in this life? Are you groaning after it?"

Why go on to perfection if you got it in conversion? Why call it perfection if it is a growth? There will be no end to growth and hence nothing to answer to the word perfection. Why groan after it if you got it in conversion? Why groan after it if it is a growth? We do not groan to grow; growth is easy, natural spontaneous.

One of the most disgusting things to me that I have ever seen in a religious service is a bishop propounding these questions to a class of Methodist preachers, and at the same time dodging the issue—trying to make it appear that they mean something else than their real meaning. It seems to me that Methodist bishops are obliged to know the real meaning and profound significance of the questions. I have heard only two or three bishops in the thirty-five annual conferences I have attended give these questions, and the things they stand for the proper application. The saintly and now sainted Bishop Lambuth was one of these. He had the experience. I have read his testimony and it had the old-time ring.

If bishops take such liberties with our doctrine and discipline what may be expected of the preachers?

It seems almost incredible that there should have been such a change in so short a time. In the former days the preacher was expected to get the experience, and preach the doctrine to others and help them into the experience, and now he is criticised, ostracised, shunned, and called a crank if he dares to preach it as the fathers did, and I suppose that those in authority would not dare say that those of us who preach the doctrine are not discriminated against.

The doctrine is clearly set forth in our church hymnal. In our old hymnal, which was ordered by the General Conference of 1886, the heading of these hymns was Entire Sanctification and Perfect Love; in the present one it is Entire Consecration and Perfect Love. In the old one there are 44 hymns on this subject, in the new one there are 26. Some of the best of Wesley's hymns on this subject have been left out of the new hymnal. I call attention to the following in the Common Hymnal: Nos. 355, 375, 371, 377, 397 and 381. I will quote stanzas 2 and 4 of 355:

> "Breathe, O breathe thy loving Spirit
> Into every troubled breast!
> Let us all in thee inherit,

> Let us find that second rest;
> Take away our bent to sinning,
> Alpha and Omega be;
> End of faith as its beginning,
> Set our hearts at liberty.
> "Finish then thy new creation,
> Pure and spotless let us be;
> Let us see thy great salvation,
> Perfectly restored in Thee;
> Changed from glory into glory,
> Till in heaven we take our place,
> Till we cast our crowns before thee,
> Lost in wonder, love and praise."

Many of these hymns are prayers and were written and sung to help the seekers after sanctification into the experience. One such is No. 375, from which I quote stanzas 2-5:

> "O that in me the sacred fire
> Might now begin to glow,
> Burn up the dross of base desire.
> And make the mountains flow.
>
> O that it now from heaven might fall
> And all my sins consume;
> Come Holy Ghost for Thee I call;
> Spirit of burning come.
>
> Refining fire go through my heart;
> Illuminate my soul;
> Scatter thy life through every part,
> And sanctify the whole.

No longer then my heart shall mourn,
While purified by grace;
I only for His glory burn,
And always see His face."

This doctrine is still in the course of study for our young preachers, although not as extensively set forth as when I took the course with Watson and Fletcher teaching, but we still have Wesley's Sermons and as long as they are in it, it will be taught; but the trend of things shows they getting it out of the course of study as fast as they can. If we don't guard carefully our colleges and universities we will have bishops and other leaders that will not only put away our doctrines of regeneration and sanctification but will fill our church with modernism. Our colleges and former university (Vanderbilt) have been the chief factors in leading our preachers away from our standards of doctrine on the subject of entire sanctification.

(This book was written 24 years ago and it is now 1949. All of Wesley's Sermons and all other books of the founders and church fathers are out of the course of study and the books of Fosdick and other liberals take their places.)

I remember that just a few years ago there was an effort on the part of certain leaders in our church to have the faith of our church recast. I suppose they were chafing a little under the fact that they were preaching one thing and the faith of the church was quite another thing. But they did not get it done. When they got a little closer down to the rank and file of the preachers of our church they saw it could not be done.

I have referred to the Zinzendorfian heresy which teaches that we are sanctified when we are converted, and am reminded of the fact that Mr. Wesley fought this erroneous doctrine vigorously wherever he went. William Bramwell declared "that he foresaw that this would be the devil's big gun," and so it has proven to be. It appears that more Methodist preachers are preaching this idea than any other. It seems strange that Methodist preachers should get so far away from their own doctrine that they would espouse one so vigorously opposed by our founder, and especially so when there is not a line in our doctrinal standards or the Bible to support it.

The only hope I have is for our church to return to the old-time power; anyone who knows our history knows the church hasn't the power it had in the early days. Just read the life and works of Wesley, Asbury, McKendree, Benjamin Abbott, Peter Cartwright, and others.

People ask today, what has become of the class meeting? I answer, it went when the testifying experience went, and will not return till that experience returns. Jesus said, "Ye shall receive power after that the Holy Ghost is come upon you, and ye shall be witnesses unto me," etc. Power and testimony go together; they are inseparable.

As for me, I am determined to preach the doctrine, testify to the experience, life the life, and be true to God and the standards of my church, which were taught me when I entered it, and to help every one I can to the better land. I have been a poor exponent of the doctrine, have blundered, lost the experience several times as John Fletcher said he did, but I am so glad that the blood has always been in reach, and that I have been enabled to touch and live.

CHAPTER V

THE DOCTRINE FROM THE STANDPOINT
OF THE BIBLE

The three dispensations, revealing the Father, the Son and the Holy Ghost, seem to indicate and foreshadow three types of piety: twilight, early morning, and noon day. The Holy Spirit in the heart and life of the church is this noon day light, and that is what the founders of Methodism preferred to call perfecton—perfect love, holiness or entire sanctification. We believe this doctrine is clearly set forth in the Bible.

Perhaps to start with we should have a good definition of sanctification. In Webster's Unabridged and International Dictionary we have it as follows:

1. To make sacred or holy; to set apart to a holy or religious use.

2. To make free from sin; to cleanse from moral corruption and pollution; to purify.

3. To make efficient the means of holiness; to render productive of holiness or piety.

4. To impart or impute sacredness, venerableness, inviolability, or the like to; to secure from violation; to give sanction to.

5. Sanctification; the act of sanctifying or making holy; also of setting apart.

So we see that sanctification does not merely mean setting apart as some folks claim, although there are some places in Scripture where it has this meaning, and sometimes the word sanctified stands for the state of salvation from sin, regeneration and the life formerly lived in sin, as in I Cor. 6:11: "And such were some of you; but now ye are washed, but ye are sanctified, but ye are justified, in the name of the Lord Jesus, and by the Spirit of our God." He had just referred to the corrupt and wicked state of the classes mentioned in verses 9 and 19 and says "such were some of you" before they had been brought into the church. There it is clear that the meaning is from a state of the world to a state of grace. I might notice the same idea in other passages, but it is not necessary; but there are many passages where the meaning is different, and we will notice a few of these.

The first passage I call attention to is I Cor. 1:30: "But now are ye in Christ Jesus who of God is made unto us, wisdom and righteousness and sanctification and redemption." I notice this text first, as it is a sort of foundation for the rest. This involves the covenant of redemption between the Father and Son, wherein the Son volunteers and undertakes the redemption of man, and the Father anoints him into a three-fold office answering to the misery that lay upon the race, the blindness of his mind, the guilt of his sin, and his captivity to Satan, as so many bars to call communion and fellowship with God and enjoyment of God; as Prophet, Priest, and King, or "wisdom, righteousness, sanctification, and redemption." Thus made to us by God the Father, all we need, our "all in all."

As Prophet he brings us the word of God, or is wisdom, this showing us our lost estate and undone condition and bringing us under conviction for sin.

As Priest he brings us pardon through the merits of his own blood, and ever intercedes for us at the Father's side. So is made unto us righteousness.

As King he is the conqueror of the whole territory of our dominion, whole nature, mind and body, casting out every preoccupying enemy, purging out every vile affection and reigning supremely there, or is our sanctification; and thus completely redeeming us from sin, and when the final battle is over the redemption of our bodies in glorification, so he is our redemption.

Another very clear passage on the subject is II Cor. 7:1: "Having therefore these promises dearly beloved, let us cleanse ourselves from all filthiness of the flesh, and spirit, perfecting holiness in the fear of God." First, we see that holiness was not completed in these (or at least a part of them) Corinthian Christians, but that it was to be accomplished in them, and the apostle is urging them on to it. It is clear that conversion had failed to bring it about, and that the process before them was not growth, as by the aid of the Holy Spirit they were to cleanse themselves. The cleansing on their part seems to have been the separation from worldly entanglements, yoked with unbelievers, chapter 6:14, 15. Also they were to cleanse themselves from all filthiness of the flesh and spirit, bringing themselves under the power of God and meeting conditions of the promises of God, chapter 6:16, 17, "And what agreement hath the temple of God with idols? For ye are the temple of the living God; as God hath said I will dwell in them and walk with them; and I will be their God and they shall be my people. Wherefore come out from among them and be ye separate, saith the Lord, and touch not the unclean thing: and I will receive you, and will be a Father unto you, and ye shall be my sons and daughters, saith the Lord Almighty."

Now the text following, and having met the conditions and obtaining the promises, God would do his work of cleansing and perfecting holiness in them.

On this passage I quote Mr. Wesley's brief explanation in his notes: "Let us cleanse ourselves (this is the latter part of the explanation which was proposed in chapter 6:1 and

resumed in verse 14) from all pollution of the flesh, all out-
ward sin, and of the spirit—all inward, yet let us not rest
in negative religion, but perfect holiness, carrying it to the
height in all its branches, and enduring to the end in all
the loving fear of God, the sure foundation of all holiness."
Dr. Adam Clarke and Dr. Watson have the same understanding of this passage, but are too lengthy to quote here.

Next we take Heb. 6:1-3: "Therefore leaving the principle of doctrine of Christ let us go on to perfection: not laying again the foundation of repentance from dead works,
and of faith toward God, of the doctrine, of baptisms, and
of laying on of hands, and of resurrection from the dead,
and of eternal judgment, and this will do if God permit." We
inquire first what principles we are to leave as we go on
unto perfection, and find that they are the foundation principles, repentance, faith, baptisms, laying on of hands,
resurrection, and the judgment; these are the foundation
of the structure of Christian character, and in order to have
a Christian character we must have these, but we are not
to stop with the foundation but go on with the building, not
to leave them out of the building but where they belong to
support the structure. Some instead of leaving them in their
places and going on with the building, kick down the foundation and go back into the world, and if ever saved must
come back and "lay again" the foundation before they begin
the building.

Others piddle around on the foundation all the time,
never get away from these rudimentary principles and so
do not go on to perfection.

We are to *go on unto perfection*, and this is not an end-
less going of ours, but as the original shows we are to be
borne or lifted into this perfection by the Holy Spirit. As to

the kind of perfection meant here the Bible is clear that at least there is a perfection in love, and there is no doubt about the Bible standard on this point. Jesus said (Matt. 5:48), "Be ye therefore perfect even as your Father in heaven is perfect," and in John 17:23 Jesus in His intercessory prayer said, "I in them and thou in me that they may be made perfect in one."

Now I observe that this was not reached in conversion, for it is held out before converted people and is attainable for them.

I note also that perfection is not attainable by growth. Perfection is one thing and maturity is quite another thing. This maturity can come only after the perfection has been attained as an experience.

Another phase of the doctrine is set forth in I Thess. 5:22-24, "Abstain from all appearance of evil, and the very God of peace sanctify you wholly; and I pray God your whole spirit and soul and body be preserved blameless unto the coming of our Lord Jesus Christ. Faithful is he that calleth you who also will do it."

Some passages show up the human agency in our sanctification more and some the divine side. First Cor. 7:1 shows up the human side, but this one emphasizes the divine side, which involves separation from all forms of worldliness, and the God of peace Himself is to sanctify them wholly every part, spirit and soul and body, and that the whole man be preserved in this state of holiness unto the coming of the Lord Jesus Christ. Then the precious promise, "Faithful is he which calleth you (to this holiness) who will do it."

I call attention to Jesus' promise of the baptism of the Holy Ghost (Acts 1:4, 5-8): "And being assembled together with them, commanded them that they should not depart from Jerusalem, but wait for the promise of the Father, which, saith he, ye have heard of me; for John truly baptized with water, but ye shall be baptised with the Holy Ghost not many days hence." "But ye shall receive power after that the Holy Ghost is come upon you and ye shall be witnesses unto me; both in Jerusalem, and in all Judea and in Samaria and unto the uttermost part of the earth." This promise was made to disciples, who were converted men and women. Some people argue that they were not converted till Pentecost, but they are ignorant of the facts; let us look at some of the facts, especially in regard to the eleven apostles. Jesus said to them, "Now ye are clean through the word which I have spoken unto you," and in His prayer for them in John 17 He says of them, "They are not of the world even as I am not of the world," verses 14 and 16 repeating it twice. He had breathed on them saying, "Receive ye the Holy Ghost," and they received a measure of the Holy Spirit, but not His fullness.

In John 14:16 Jesus said, "I will pray the Father and he shall give you another Conforter that he may abide with you forever; even the Spirit of Truth: whom the world cannot receive because it seeth him not neither knoweth him, but ye know him, for he dwelleth with you and shall be in you." In the 17th chapter of John this promised prayer is recorded, and in this prayer He prayed for their sanctification (verses 17-23), and not only for theirs but for all who should believe on him through their word. That meant for all believers down to the end of the age. How glad I am that He included me in that gracious prayer.

Now we will turn over to the second chapter of Acts and see how the prayer was answered and the promise fulfilled—verses 1-4: "And when the day of Pentecost was fully come they were all with one accord in one place.

"And suddenly there came a sound from heaven, as of a rushing mighty wind, and it filled all the house where they were sitting.

"And there appeared unto them cloven tongues as of fire, and it sat upon each of them.

"And they were all filled with the Holy Ghost and began to speak with other tongues as the Spirit gave them utterance."

Another case of the baptism of the Holy Ghost upon believers is recorded in Acts 8:15-17: "Who when they were come down, prayed for them, that they might receive the Holy Ghost; (for as yet he was fallen on none of them: only they were baptized in the name of the Lord Jesus). Then laid they their hands upon them, and they received the Holy Ghost.

One other case of the Holy Ghost's baptism on converted people is given in Acts 19:1-7, which let the reader see, as it is rather long to quote here, but which with the other passages quoted above show clearly that the baptism of the Holy Ghost is for believers only, and is the same thing as entire sanctification.

I notice only one more passage of Scripture, which bears another aspect of this subject (I Peter 1:2): "Elect according to the foreknowledge of God the Father through sanctification of the Spirit, unto obedience and sprinkling of the blood of Jesus Christ." Here is the doctrine of election and the doctrine of sanctification set forth in their proper relation to each other. This tells (with verse one) who the elect are and how they are made, also the result in the life of the elected sanctified ones.

Who they are: "Strangers scattered throughout Pontus, Galatia, Capadocia, Asia and Bithynia, Elect." These strangers were the saints who were scattered abroad by the persecution in the earlier days of the church and the converts in the different provinces. Their election was according to the foreknowledge of God the Father, by or through sanctification of the Spirit, showing how this election is accomplished. God has not only foreknowledge, but has foreordained that only those who would accept His Son and trust the merits of His blood can be elected, and every one who does this is elected, and every one who fails to do this is rejected.

These elected sanctified ones are brought into obedience and sprinkling of the blood of Jesus Christ. This is the great need of the church today, obedience and holiness, and they belong together and are absolutely inseparable. We may want to be perfect in obedience, but we are lacking in the inward power without sanctification which brings us unto obedience and under the sprinkled, or sprinkling blood cleanses and keeps us clean, while the Holy Spirit empowers for obedience, the obedience we have longed for before but were not able to render it.

Thousands of people bear witness today to this very thing. The idea is not that we get sprinkled with blood and then go on away from it forgetting about it, but it is a living under the sprinkling bood, on the altar and under the blood, is the idea in this text. A good woman testifying to this experience in meeting one day said, "I am a pebble in the brook." This was very expressive of the true idea, ever being cleansed and kept clean. The word is the channel, the blood is the stream, and the Holy Spirit is the administrator and guide.

There are more places in the Scripture that teach entire sanctification than there are that teach regeneration, but this paper is getting longer than I intended it should.

CHAPTER VI

PERSECUTION OF HOLINESS AND
HOLINESS PREACHERS

Definition: Holiness is a definite second work of grace, wrought in the heart by the Holy Spirit, subsequent to justification, by the application of the blood of Jesus which "cleanses from all sin." I John 1:7, the remains of inbred sin, enabling one to love God with all the hearts, soul, mind, and strength, and thy neighbor as thy self.

This is called by the Rev. John Wesley, "The second blessing," not a second blessing, but "The second blessing." He coined the expression: do not criticise it unless you mean to belittle him.

Persecution of holiness is a true mark of a fallen church. The world doesn't persecute. It was true with Cain killing his brother because his own works were evil and his brother's righteous—acceptable to God. I John 3:12.

It was true with the false prophets and Jeremiah. It was true with other prophets who stood for the truth of God. It was true when the Roman Catholic church persecuted Madam Guyon, Archbishop Fenelon and St. Francis of Assisi. It was true with the bishops and clergy in England when they persecuted John Wesley.

The more men persecute holiness and holiness preachers, the more they display the need of the thing they persecute. I knew a preacher who was quite a critic of the second blessing, and yet he had a dirty spot in his life that caused him to get out of the ministry, when if he had sought and obtained what he was criticising, it would have saved him.

It has been true in the modern holiness movement especially in the Methodist Church since it slid away from the Methodist doctrine and there is not an *honest, intel-*

ligent man in the church who can and will deny it.

Antiholiness men on examining commitees in Conference make it hard on young holiness men coming into the Conference. Seems they want to brow beat them out. Assuming an antagonistic and criticising attitude toward them. How little, cowardly, and unbecoming men in authority.

There are three classes of Methodist preachers today with regard to the doctrine of holiness.

1. There are those who have the experience and love and preach the doctrine.

2. There are those who do not seem to have committed themselves to the doctrine or declared against it, a sort of middlegrounders. Seeing the truth they cannot afford to fight it, but not willing to pay the price to obtain it.

3. The third class are antiholiness preachers; they hate the doctrine, and persecute the preachers and members who stand for it. Some of these are leaders of the church, bishops, district superintendents, professors in schools of religion; some will want to deny this, but they need not deny it. I know it is true. I have been not only seeing it for about forty years but have been the victim of it myself and others who were not quite so stout-hearted as I, left the church because of this persecution. All these preachers assured the church that they were going to have the experience of sanctification —Christian perfection, at the door of the Conference, when they took the solemn vows to go on to perfection, expected it in this life. And were groaning after it; and as soon as they had gotten in, they proceeded to join those who were persecuting those who profess to have received what they had just said they were going to have.

No bishop, preacher, or Conference can make that expression in Heb. 6:1 and in these solemn vows "go on toward," it is "going on TO," or, literally in the original, *be born on into* for it is a work of the Holy Spirit to bear us into the experience just as he does into justification.

Why do they persecute the holiness preachers? They do not persecute the preachers who run after worldly sports, ball games, movies and theatres, or those who have, after their vows to the church to abstain from the use of tobacco, go on using it. No, the only ones they persecute are the holiness preachers, so holiness is more hateful to them than sin.

A church in this Conference, I am told, which had holiness preachers for a number of years and most of them believed in it, asked for a pastor who preached it and the district superintendent said, "No, I will not send a holiness preacher there." One can surmise why. The district superintendent no doubt had cabinet help in such a purpose. They want to stamp it out. That is the plan that has been used during these forty or fifty years by the antiholiness leadership. Some of the antiholiness leaders in Dr. H. C. Morrison's Conference turned him out of the Conference, not because he had done anything wrong, but because he had gone to hold a revival where some one objected to it, but before the meeting of his Annual Conference, they met and rescinded the act.

Dr. Morrison was to help one of the pastors of the Northern Church in a revival meeting, the arrangements were made, and the pastor told his district superintendent about it, and he said, "No. You cannot have that man here." That, of course, settled it; but there was a little holiness church nearby which, when the pastor found that Dr. Morrison could not come to the Methodist church, said let him come to our church, which he did. And in that meeting a young man was converted named E. Stanley Jones, and after his wonderful conversion Stanley said, "Now I have to preach and I have no education. Where must I go to school?" Dr. Morrison said, "We will take you to Asbury College." He went, and the first year was sanctified, and graduated and thus the foundation was laid well for the wonderful life of the greatest and most outstanding preacher in the world today; known and loved around the world. Dr. Morrison was the greatest preacher so far as soul winning and blessing the people of these United States of any preacher in the country; but where is the poor little district superintendent? Only a few people know his name.

No one can fight this work of the Holy Spirit and prosper; the church that tolerates this persecution cannot prosper.

My worst enemies for 30 or 40 years have been Methodist preachers and it is true today. These antiholiness preachers will not let me preach in their pulpits if they can help it. I have held the church in all my charges, staying four years in a great many of them, and have kept the church from dividing in at least two places, but the preachers are my enemies. In one town a man and his wife who had borne half the burden in building the Methodist church, professed santification. A Holiness evangelist went to the town and set up his tent and a great many professed to be saved and a good number professed sanctification. I went in and helped the evangelist in altar work and otherwise; the leading lawyer in the town was converted and other leading people. The antiholiness pastor of the Methodist church pitched in to fighting holiness; a larger number of the holiness people began to take steps to build them a church and to go into the holiness movement, and I went over to see them and kept them from doing it. I told them the Methodist church was a holiness church and maybe the next pastor would preach it. So they stopped and that kept them from dividing the church.

Soon after this I moved into a charge where a lot of our leading members were paying a holiness preacher to come to a school house in the community and preach; the pastor before me would not let him preach in the church and fought holiness, so I found them on the verge of division and the establishment of a holiness church. I did not fight him or refer to him at all. I went on preaching our own doctrine and in a few months I was visiting in the home of one of our stewards and the wife said to me: "I just told Papa there was no use for us to be paying a man to come here to preach what our own preacher was preaching." So he stopped coming and that ended the division.

They say that holiness preaching divides the church; that is true, the Gospel is a divisive element; Jesus said it would divide homes, array parents against the children and children against parents, and his preaching and the work divided the Jewish church; some believed and some rejected him. The preaching of the apostles divided the believers from the unbelievers but the antiholiness preacher's preaching does not seem to divide anything; they just let them all go along the broad road together and some of the preachers run with them to the things of the world, sports, movies, etc.

But I am asking in all seriousness, why do they persecute the holiness preachers? Why don't they take them up and try them for heresy if they are not preaching the Bible and the Methodist doctrines? That is the Bible way and the best way to get rid of them, not go along snobbing, criticising and discriminating against them.

How many times in the bishop's cabinet when one of the holiness preacher's names comes up for appointment, has one of the cabinet members objected to an appointment of this brother to a certain charge, saying: "Bishop, this is a good man, but he is cranky on holiness and it will not do to send him to this charge." The bishop hears the objection, and agrees; the brother is reserved for hard scrabble missions.

Let us look at this action of the cabinet. Will it bear the light of good, sound reasoning, to say nothing of the attitude of brotherly love? Is this not virutally arresting or assailing the ministerial character of this brother? They will not bring him up in Conference and try him; but they knife him in the back in the cabinet. He cannot defend himself. The brother is sent to hard scrabble mission; do not the people of hardscrabble deserve protection from an imposter or an unsafe man as much as the other charge? Is the interest in the people of both charges the question at stake or is it the salary? You see you are forced to the conclusion that it is the salary. It is not the work done, as the holiness preachers do as good or better work than others and this is generally conceded. One of the presiding elders of the former M. E. Church, South, was asked why he got so many of the holiness preachers in his district. He said, "Because they do better work than the others." That elder was outspoken W. A. Newell, and all know he was not a very strong sympathizer with holiness.

So it is easily seen that the holiness preacher goes out to the short grazing; they see to it that he does not get to the fat pasture. That is one reason we get such a large per cent of our preachers and most spiritual members, even in the city churches from the country and mill villages; these men who hold revivals and preach the whole Gospel are doing their work out there. I got four preachers out of one revival out of about a hundred and thirty conversions in one country church. Two of them are preaching and another graduated at Duke and is supposed to be preaching. I got two more out of a small school house revival from one family.

I ask again, why don't they "take him up and turn him out and let the church roll on?" I answer that most of them are intelligent enough to know that they can't do it; they know that these holiness men are preaching the Methodist doctrine. Many anti-holiness men are bitter enough to turn them out if they could work up a cause but they know they can't do it.

The thing has happened that John Wesley said he was afraid would happen. He said that he was not afraid that the time would come when there would be no Methodist church, but he was afraid that it would exist only in form and without the power.

The church is even losing its form in some respects. In the bishop's address to the General Conference in 1824 they said: "If Methodists give up the doctrine of entire sanctification, or suffer it to become a dead letter, *we are a fallen people.* Holiness is the main cord that binds us together; relax this and you loosen the whole system."

In 1847 in the bishop's address they said: "Extensive revivals of religion have crowned the labors of our preachers, and the life-giving energy of the Gospel in the conversion of sinners and *sanctification of believers* has been seldom more apparent among us. The boon of Wesleyan Methodism as we received it from the fathers has not been forfeited in our hands." This was signed by Bishops Paine, Pierce, Kavanaugh, Wightman, Marvin, Doggett, McTyeire and Keener.

In 1894 the bishops' address says: "The privilege of believers to attain unto a state of entire sanctification, or perfect love, and to abide therein is a well known teaching of

Methodism. Witnesses to this experience have never been wanting in the church, though few in comparison with the whole membership. Among them have been men and women of beautiful consistency and seraphic ardor, jewels of the church. Let the doctrine still be preached and the experience still be testified."

These addresses continued in much the same way for a number of years but this is the latest I have a record of, but this is enough to show that it is and has been the doctrine of the church from the beginning.

Dr. Lovic Pierce made the statement just before his death in a little book on sanctification that "In the first twenty years of my ministry 95% of our people were all alive and awake to this full salvation idea and pressing it, and often finding it as manifestly as they did conversion; but now in the 74th year of my ministry 75% of our members are living in indifference to entire sanctification, not believing in it, praying for it, or desiring it."

He joined Conference in 1804 and preached 75 years, which would bring him up to 1879 which covers the larger period of the decline of this doctrine and experience.

Are these preachers who persecute their brethren for preaching the known doctrine of our church worthy of the highest respect and confidence of the church and the public generally?

I ask again, why do some Methodist preachers persecute other Methodist preachers for preaching holiness when it is the chief cornerstone of the Methodist faith? The Wesleys got the doctrines of justification by faith and the winess of the spirit from the Moravians; but they resurrected and repossessed the doctrine of holiness and so it is the main distinguishing doctrine of the Methodist church.

Persecution of the holiness preachers has driven some

of the most useful men out of the church. "Uncle" Bud Robinson was a circuit rider in the church in Texas and at one of the annual conferences his report was as follows. Bishop Goodsell presided, and Bud said, "Bishop, during the year I have visited and prayed in 1,426 homes and in revivals have seen over 1,600 souls converted and sanctified." The bishop was amazed and said, "Brethren, what Brother Robinson has reported in conversions is more than a whole conference in the east reported."

Dr. George C. Wise at the funeral of "Uncle" Bud gave the following facts: two million miles traveled, thirty-three thousand sermons preached, a hundred thousand souls at his altars, having labored with seventy-three denominations; he had spent around eighty-five thousand dollars to help educate young people for Christian work; he had written fourteen books and had sold more than a half million of them; he had secured for his own church paper fifty-three thousand and thirty-eight subscribers.

And yet this highly useful man was frozen out of the Methodist church by persecution; but he has helped to established and press the work in one of the greatest soul saving agencies in our land today—the Nazarene Church— which stands for a whole Bible and all the doctrines of the original Methodist church.

I saw statistics of the Nazarene church a few years ago which showed the marvelous growth it was making. The amounts of their offerings made in comparison with the M. E. Church, South, showed that they gave about seven times as much per member as the Methodists. They are tithers and while most of them are the "common people," they do not support shows, movies, ball games, tobacco factories, etc., but do support the kingdom of heaven.

From our own W. N. C. Conference went a good preacher and evangelist to bless the Nazarene church, Rev. Raymond Browning, because of this same persecution.

This glorious doctrine and experience is essential to real evangelism. I have tested it out in my ministerial life of 62 years. I preached about ten years before receiving it, and had some success in revival work but not like it was afterward.

As a result of the preaching of this glorious truth in the Gospel I have preached during the forty-seven years of my traveling ministry, God has given me about six thousand conversions, three thousand and fifty-three additions to the church, the baptism of nine hundred and nine adults, and eight hundred and fourteen infants, which baptisms were mainly results of the revivals God has given me. In one charge, the Mooresville circuit, during my four years there, I received about six hundred members, baptized three hundred and thirty-six infants and forty-four adults, and had more than twelve hundred professions of religion.

Our preachers would do well to read the history of the working of this great doctrine and experience in early American Methodism, in the life of Asbury, Peter Cartwright, Benjamin Abbot and other in the days of the camp meetings and see how prominent this doctrine and experience was in them and in the annual conferences; and then in the later years with our great evangelists, Rev. Beverly Cardine, D.D., Dr. H. C. Morrison, Dr. J. B. Culpepper, Dr. C. F. Wimberly, Sam P. Jones and others. In fact, nearly all the great evangelists had the experience and preached the doctrine.

What is the matter with our modern preachers in our large churches not even trying to have revivals, with thousands of lost souls all about them going down to hell; they seem to be entirely indifferent about it; they remind me of the little dog which lay on the ox's hay, he would not eat the hay himself and would not let the ox eat it. They will not hold revivals themselves and will not let anyone who could and would hold them do it. A fearful responsibility to face some time, most of them *"holding down"* fat jobs and they do not want any one to "rock the boat," and a good many of them fighting holiness.

I have heard our beloved and now sainted Bishop E. D. Mouzon say more than once that he believed all the Methodist doctrines from prevenient grace to perfect love; and he told one of the presiding elders who perhaps knew him better and was closer to him than any other, that we should never have let the Nazarenes get away from us, that we needed them and what they had to carry on with; and he said many times, "Brother, I am done with sin."

I am indicting modernism as the enemy that through persecution and other means pushed out the founders of the Nazarenes, and many others of the holiness branches of the church; and they have not only opposed holiness, but are in the same way persecuting those who stand for a real experience of justification as it gets in their way. Peter describes them minutely in II Peter 2 and Jude in verses 3:19; in verse 3 he warns all to contend earnestly for the faith which was once delivered unto the saints; then proceeds to tell about those who have crept in unawares "Denying the only Lord God and our Lord Jesus Christ."

This modernism has wrecked Germany; introduced into Germany about 75 years ago in their schools, soon went into the churches, law, medicine and all the institutions where their educated men operated and the world sees some of the awful results today. Out of Germany has come the worst form of militarism, nazism, modernism and nudism, which they tried to put into England but English laws would not allow nudism; but France did welcome it and from France and Germany it has come to America and a number of states allow it, and this foot of the beast has its tracks in our once fair land, polluting certain territories where officers and people love to have it so.

Leaders of our educational institutions went to Germany about 50 and 60 years ago and topped off with what they called "the higher criticism," and began putting it into our schools and it has spread to about all of them except the holiness institutions which have fought it constantly.

What is the faith, or lack of faith, of the modernists in the Bible and Christianity? It consists in the unbelief in and denial of the five fundamental teachings of the Bible, viz.: The Bible account of the creation and fall of man, the divine inspiration of the Holy Scriptures, the Virgin birth, diety and Godhead of Jesus, the blood atonement, and the bodily resurrection of Jesus. Now when you take these out of the Bible, what have you left?

These modernists are teaching in our schools, preaching in our pulpits, and some of them writing in our Sunday school literature, teaching the youth of the Methodist church. The fact is that they have the management of the church at the present time, and few men are raising their voices against it notwithstanding the vows of the Methodist preachers "to do all in our power to drive away all erroneous and strange doctrines."

Brother Bud Robinson told in one of his books of one of these modernistic pastors, a D.D. in the Methodist church in a city where he was holding a meeting, who called for Brother Bud to come over to the parsonage; Brother Bud went, the preacher questioned him about his preaching and then said he respected Brother Bud, but that his preaching was all a matter of ignorance, that he had no such experience of conversion, or sanctification, that he had been born right and trained into it and, turning to his two little children, said those children were pure, born right and were being trained right. Brother Bud went on about his work, and it was not long until this same D.D. got drunk and took in the town, then sent up his credentials to his presiding elder. No, he did not have the things Uncle Buddie was preaching; he knew nothing about them; his modernism had left them out.

I would not have the junk in my head and life that these modernists are putting into many of our young preachers for anything in the world.

The devil had been attacking the church for the ages by atheism, deism, universalism, etc., but could accomplish little. Finally he saw his mistake, that he was working only from the outside, so he managed to get on the inside in the form of modernism and as a fifth columnist he is succeeding wonderfully well, as he corrupts the ministry and teaching forces of the church and substitutes these for real salvation.

CHAPTER VII

THE DOCTRINE FROM THE STANDPOINT OF EXPERIENCE

Experience; what is it?

First. It often refers to a judgment derived from experience in the primary sense by reasoning from that in combination with other data.

Second: In philosophy experience in its strict sense to what has occurred in a person's own knowledge and of course relates to the past alone as what a person has suffered from some disease or other unpleasant thing, or what he has enjoyed from pleasant association.

Locke, the celebrated philosopher, in his essay on the human understanding assigns experience as the only universal source of human knowledge. Whence hath the mind all the materials of reason and knowledge? To this I answer in one word, from experience; in that all our knowledge is founded, and from that ultimately derives itself.

In religion experience means knowledge gained by trial or practice. The man unacquainted with those spiritual changes described in the Bible can have no correct notion of them. He may have some idea of the possibilities of the change indicated by regeneration, sanctification, etc., but cannot understand their nature; they are foolishness unto them. The unregenerate man cannot go beyond experience and understand that gracious work and state, neither can a regenerated man who has not been sanctified go beyond experience and understand sanctification, and just so can none of us understand the experience of glorification or resurrection glory till we experience it. This being true I pass at once to the consideration of the experience of entire sanctification or perfect love. It is an experience just as definite, just as profound, just as distinct, and just as satisfying to the seekers as regeneration is to the one who seeks and finds it, and just as far beyond the understanding of the justified man as regeneration is beyond the understanding of the unsaved man, so that neither are competent to pass upon that which they have not experienced.

Before introducing the witness to this experience I want to say a word in regard to testifying to the experience. David said, "Come and hear all ye who fear God, and I will declare what he hath done for my soul." Jesus said, Acts 1:8, "But ye shall receive power after that the Holy Ghost is come upon you, and you shall be witnesses unto me." Rev. 12:11, "And they overcame him by the blood of the Lamb and the word of their testimony." So the privilege and duty of testimony are very clear. But there is a proper time and place as well as a proper manner for testimony. We are not to cast our pearls before swine, but at the proper time and before the proper ones these pearls are suitably appreciated and we then can glorify God through testimony.

The manner of our testifying is very important. We are not to boast of anything we are, or have, or have done, or can do, but we are to make our boast in the Lord—magnify Him, His grace and His love. The motive for our testimony should be to glorify God and help others. We should not testify even for our own pleasure. The testimony of the man whom Jesus healed who had been blind is a good example of testimony to his marvelous grace. He was humble, steadfast, persistent and courageous in his testimony not flinching under fire of cross examination and persecution of his and Jesus' enemies; but held to his testimony and after suffering excommunication for it, Jesus met him and gave him another and greater blessing, revealing Himself more fully to him.

I want now to introduce some witnesses to the experience of entire sanctification.

John Fletcher, one of the great preachers and writers among the early Methodist fathers, in giving his experience of holiness, said: "Last Monday evening he (God) spoke to me by these words, 'Reckon yourself therefore to be dead indeed unto sin but alive unto God through Jesus Christ, our Lord.' I obeyed the voice of God. I now obey it, and tell you all to the praise of His love. I am free from sin, dead unto sin, and alive unto God. I received the blessing four or five times before, but I lost it by not observing the order of God, who tells us with the heart man believeth unto righteousness and with his mouth confession is made unto salvation. Now my brethren, you see my folly. I have confessed it in your presence and now I am resolved before you all to confess my Master. I will confess him to all the world; and I will declare unto you in the presence of the Holy Trinity I am now dead indeed, unto sin, and alive unto God through Jesus Christ, who is my indwelling holiness, my all in all." Rev. Joseph Benton, the well known commentator and intimate friend of Fletcher, says that after this profession of holiness that although he was of a naturally fiery temper, so much so that before this profession he would oftentimes throw himself on the floor and lie there most of the night imploring victory over his own temper, but after this he was never known out of temper. Others writing of him confirm Mr. Benson's statements.

Next I will introduce Bishop Whatcoat. He says: "My faith and love grew stronger and stronger, but I soon found that though I was justified freely, yet I was not sanctified wholly. This rought me into a deep concern, and confirmed

my resolution to admit of no peace or truce with the devil
which I still found in my heart. I was sensible that they
both hindered me at present in my holy exercises and that
I could not enter into the joy of my Lord unless they were
all rolled out. After many sharp and painful conflicts and
many gracious visitations also on the 28th of March, 1761,
my soul was drawn out and egaged in a manner it never was
before. Suddenly I was stripped of all but love, and in this
happy state, rejoicing evermore and in everything giving
thanks, I continued for some years with little intermission or
abatement, wanting nothing for soul or body more than I
received from day to day."

Next we will hear from Miss Frances E. Willard, one of
the greatest American women—great when seen from any
angle. She says: "In 1866, Mrs. Bishop Hamilton came to
our village, and we were closely associated in the work of
the American Ladies' Centennial Association that built Hick
Hall. This saintly woman placed in my hands the life of
Hester Ann Rogers, Life of Carvosso, Life of Mrs. Fletcher,
Wesley's Sermon on Christian Perfection, and Mrs. Palmer's
Guide to Holiness. I had never seen any of these books before, but had read Peck's Central Idea of Christianity and
had been greatly interested in it. I also heard saintly testi-
monies in prayer meetings, and in a general way believed
in the doctrine of holiness. But my reading these books, my
talks and prayers with Mrs. Hamilton, that modern Mrs.
Fletcher, deeply impressed me. I began to desire and pray
for holiness of heart. Soon after this Dr. and Mrs. Phoebe
Palmer came to Evanston as guests of Mrs. Hamilton, and
for weeks they held meetings in our church. This was in
the winter of 1866, the precise date I cannot give. One
evening early in the meetings when Mrs. Palmer had spoken
with marvelous clearness and power and at the close those

desirous of entering into the higher Christian life had been asked to kneel at the altar, another crisis came to me. (The first had been at the time of her conversion previously noted). It was not so tremendous as the first, but it was one that deeply left its impress on my spirit . . . kneeling in utter self-abandonment, I consecrated myself anew to God. I cannot describe the deep welling up of joy that gradually possessed me. I was utterly free from care; I was blithe as a bird that is good for nothing except to sing . . . The conscious emotional presence of Christ through the Holy Spirit held me. I ran about upon His errands just for love. Life was a halcyon day. All my friends knew and noticed the change, and I would not like to write down the lovely things some of them said to me, but they did me no harm for I was shut in with the Lord. Since then I have sat at the feet of every teacher of holiness I could reach, have read their books and campared their views. I love and reverence and am greatly drawn to all and never feel out of harmony with their spirit. Wonderful uplifts come to me as I pass on— clearer views of the life of God in the soul of man. Indeed, it is the only life, and all my being sets toward it as the river toward the sea. Celestial things grow dearer to me; the love of Christ is steadfast in my soul; the habitudes of a disciple sit more easily upon me; tenderness toward humanity and lower order of beings increase with the years; in the temperance labor and woman's questions I see the stirring of Christ's heart; in the comradeship of Christian work my spirit takes delight and prayer has become my atmosphere."

Next we will hear from Mr. D. L. Moody. He says: "The blessing came upon me suddenly like a flash of lightning. For months I had been hungering and thirsting for power in service. I had come to that point that I think I had died if I had not got it. I remember I was walking the streets of New York. I had no more heart in the business I was about than if I had not belonged to the world at all. Right there on the street the power of God seemed to come upon me so wonderfully that I had to ask God to stay his hand. I was filled with a sense of God's goodness, and felt as though I could take the whole world to my heart. I took the old sermon I had preached before without any power; it was the same old truth but there was a new power. Many were impressed and converted. This happened years after I was converted myself."

Testifying to substantially the same thing and in much the same way are many men and women not only of the generations past but at the present time, not only in the Methodist churches but in other churches. I might give the experience of Madam Guyon, Charles G. Finney, George Muller, Drs. Gordon, Earl, Levy and others of the Baptist Church; Drs. Carradine, Godbey, T. H. B. Anderson, Fisk, Schoolfield, and many more, as well as many of the best men of today. The doctrine is not dead nor the experience a thing of the past, and one of the most hopeful things of the present is that these Spirit-filled men and women are getting souls saved and sanctified, and many of the young preachers coming into the work are converted under such preaching and holiness fighters haven't much influence with them, and these will carry on the glorious work.

Now what can be said against a thing, anything, with such a cloud of witnesses testifying to it, and especially such witnesses as I have introduced here—real witnesses testifying from first-hand knowledge—not what some one else said, but what they had felt and seen with confidence telling. This testimony is of the most positive character, coming from the best and holiest men and women, not of a single age or period of the church's history, but in every age.

What shall we say of men who criticise, ridicule and make light of a fact so well attested and established as this doctrine and experience? Yea, what shall we say of those who refuse to believe such an array of testimony? I will say for one that I would not want such a man on the jury that would have to try me in the courts. Such unbelief is willful and inexcusable.

The critics of our doctrine and experience of holiness remind me of the story of the Campbellite preacher who went into a new community and preached a sermon against the idea of experimental religion and proved to his way of thinking, and so satisfied was he that it could not be met by any one present that he threw out the challenge: "If anyone has anything to say to what I have said let him speak" and took his seat. No one moved. Finally an old Negro on the back seat arose and began slowly to formuate his answer, saying: "You say da's no sich thing as 'sperimental 'ligion. Now s'pose we change it jus' a little and say da's no sich thing as 'sperimental 'ligion dat is as you knows uv." All the theologians in the country could not have beaten it.

I have for some time felt it my duty to write this series of articles, in which I earnestly contend for the faith once delivered to the saints, in which I defend the doctrine of our church, and by which I trust at least some of the saints will be edified and encouraged.

CHAPTER VIII

How to Obtain the Blessing

I. The first thing in order to obtain the blessing of entire sanctification is to find the doctrine set forth in the Bible as Mr. Wesley says he found it in the Scriptures, and this we will do when we search them with unveiled eyes desiring to know the truth which sets men free, the whole will of God.

II. The second thing is to feel the need in our hearts, and this need is felt by every truly regenerated person, a hunger for something not yet attained, a longing for the fullness of the blessing of the gospel of Christ, or the baptism of the Holy Spirit. Not only are we to feel this need, but to have the assurance that we are born again and that all our sins are blotted out: for it is as sons having the "birth-right" that we are entitled to the "blessing." Let us be clear here, or we will not be clear anywhere.

III. Having the witness of the Spirit that we are the children of God, we are then in position to make the next step which is entire consecration, and this must include all we are or hope to be, all we have or hope to have, all surrendered for sacrifice or service, to be anything, to go anywhere, or do anything that He wills, and our wills wholly surrendered as the climax of the sacrifice. Let the whole being cry out, "O Lord I am wholly thine and thine forever."

IV. When we are assured in our own hearts that we have made the consecration, that it is complete, then we are ready for next step which is faith. We are sanctified by faith. Acts 26:18. We are here to believe "all things are possible to him that believeth." We must not put feelings before faith, faith goes before feelings. We cannot feel it until it is a fact, and it cannot be a fact until we believe for it, believe, keep on believing, not merely that He will, but that He does sanctify you now.

V. Then we are ready for the fifth and final step which is confession; faith and confession go together and must stay together. "With the heart man believeth unto righteousness and with the mouth confession is made unto salvation." Rom. 10:10. "They overcame him (the devil) by the blood of the Lamb, and the word of their testimony." Rev. 12:11.

Remember, we may not be confessing to feeling but to faith, the confession is the stand we take on or by faith, and the faith is on the word of God that cannot fail.

Take this stand and remain firm and feelings will take care of themselves.

CHAPTER IX

A Brief Personal Sketch

I was born into this world January 4, 1866, about three miles below Franklin, N. C. I was born again in Franklin in the Methodist Church, March 11, 1884. I learned of my first birth from my parents and the records, although I was there I do not remember it and had to be told by others of the important event, but of the latter birth no one had to tell me about it; yes, I was there and knew it. "I know the time, I know the place" and all the devils in hell and all the men on earth cannot make me doubt that I was born again. (It was about 10 years before I got settled in the experience of sanctification; got the experience four or five times and lost it by not testifying to it, as John Finch did.)

It was in an old-time revival meeting where it occurred; the meeting was conducted by Rev. Wm. A. Thomas, the pastor, and Rev. J. H. Weaver, the P. E. It continued three weeks and I was the last one converted, had been sick and under conviction the whole three weeks and had been promising the Lord if he would let me get to the meeting that I would seek him, so the last night I got to go and was graciously saved.

I soon felt called to preach and under the guidance of these two old time God-called preachers I was soon started in the ministry, two years an exhorter, and sixty-two years preaching have followed; they have been glorious years to me. I was a traveling preacher forty-seven years, have been retired eleven years and have been busy teaching the older ladies' class in the first Methodist Church in Lenoir, and preaching occasionally. Since retiring I have a little shop in my basement in which I make odd pieces of furniture and other things. I have passed my ninety-second birthday.

I have recently been writing some pamphlets and folders, putting some of my tithe money into these publications trying to do all the good I can.

There are some repetitions in this book but I think the setting in which they are made justifies the repetition.

o o o

Since the publication of the third edition of this book in 1949, many things have taken place: My first wife, who had been an helpmeet indeed, helping in the work for fifty-seven years, died and the Lord has given me another wonderful companion, she has typed my tracts, sermons, booklets including some earlier ones. We have gotten out more than one hundred fifty of these and an estimated 275,000 have been printed and gone out or going out free.

In my basement shop I have made almost every kind of furniture and many of the wood-working machines. I have furnished two or three small shops with machines for making furniture.

Best of all is my Bible class that has an enrollment of about 75, and we have an attendance of between thirty and forty each Friday evening in my home. Often we have visitors come in to study with us; this pleases us very much. We have been going for almost three years and have gone through the Old Testament and Matthew of the New Testament. This at my age of ninety-two is giving me real joy and makes me feel that, "Bringing forth fruit in old age" can be done.

There has developed a spirit of friendship and devotion for each other that makes us feel like we were one large family. We are making the Bible central in our lives, homes and for the community.